CONTENTS

CHEETAHS IN DANGER

Cheetahs are the sprinters of the animal world! They are the fastest animals on land. They can run up to 110 kilometres per hour (70 mph) over short distances. Unfortunately, they cannot run fast enough to escape dangers from people.

Cheetah losses

People with guns and traps have killed many cheetahs. In 1900, there were more than 100,000 cheetahs in the wild. Today, only around 10,000 cheetahs remain. There are so few cheetahs still living in the wild that they are in danger of becoming **extinct**.

Cheetahs have long legs and slim bodies, which are built for speed.

Animal SOS!

SAVE THE
CHEETAH

Louise Spilsbury

Raintree is an imprint of Capstone Global Library Limited, a company incorporated in England and Wales having its registered office at 264 Banbury Road, Oxford, OX2 7DY – Registered company number: 6695582

www.raintree.co.uk
myorders@raintree.co.uk

Produced for Raintree by Calcium Creative Ltd
Editors for Calcium Creative Ltd: Sarah Eason and Rachel Blount
Designer: Emma DeBanks
Printed and bound in India

ISBN 978 1 4747 9767 2 (hardback)
ISBN 978 1 4747 9769 6 (paperback)

British Library Cataloguing in Publication Data
A full catalogue records for this book is available from the British Library.

Acknowledgements
Cover: Shutterstock: Stu Porter. Inside: Dreamstime: Chriskruger 16, Dimaberkut 24, Doughnuts64 12, Flatscreen 11, Francois6 19, Hedrus 28, Kaphotokevm1 1, 29, Kurtnielsen 10, Madd 25, Ryzhov 27, Schmali666 8, Tank_bmb 20, Unique2109 14, Wizreist 26; Shutterstock: Bryan Busovicki 6, Fitzsimage 23, Geraldb 17, Javarman 14, Daleen Loest 18, Francois Loubser 21, Stu Porter 4, 5, Steve Price 22, Jerome Scholler 9, Nickolay Stanev 7, Gary C. Tognoni 15.

Every effort has been made to contact copyright holders of material reproduced in this book. Any omissions will be rectified in subsequent printings if notice is given to the publisher.

Meet the cheetah

Cheetahs are magnificent animals. These big cats have honey-coloured fur with black spots. They have small heads, a long body and long, powerful legs. When cheetahs run, they use their long tails to help them steer and turn in the direction they want to go, like the **rudder** of a boat.

Cheetahs are so speedy they could run alongside a car on the motorway!

RESCUE THE CHEETAH!

Be informed! Find out all you can about magnificent cheetahs and their way of life. Reading this book is a good way to start!

CHEETAHS IN THE WILD

Cheetahs live mainly in grasslands. These are large, flat areas of land covered in dry grasses. Cheetahs also live in rocky hills and places with scattered, bushy plants. Nearly all of the cheetahs that still remain in the wild live in Africa.

Vanishing cheetahs

Cheetahs once lived in almost all parts of Africa and throughout Asia. Sadly, these amazing creatures are now extinct in 25 countries where they once lived. Today, they are found only in parts of eastern, central and south-western Africa, and in a small area in Iran.

Cheetahs can see **prey** from far across open grasslands.

Living on the grasslands

Cheetahs travel long distances over open land, looking for food. **Males** live in groups of two or three animals, usually brothers. **Females** live alone, except when they have cubs. Cheetahs roam the grasslands hunting for animals such as hares, wildebeest calves and gazelles.

ANIMAL SOS!

In Asia, cheetahs are nearly extinct. Today, there are only 60 to 100 cheetahs left in Iran. There are still a few small groups of cheetahs living in parts of north-eastern Iran.

Cheetahs watch prey from the long, dry grass.

CHEETAH ENEMY

In the past, humans hunted and trapped cheetahs. People trained the cheetahs to hunt animals for them, such as antelopes. They also killed cheetahs for their beautiful, spotted skins. Owning cheetah skins showed that people were wealthy and important.

Danger from poachers

Today, there are laws to stop people from hunting cheetahs. However, some **poachers** still trap these lovely wild cats. Poachers are people who catch cheetahs illegally. They mainly catch cheetah cubs. Poachers sell them as pets or for their fur. Many of these cubs die when they are transported long distances in cramped cages.

Cheetahs look and listen for danger.

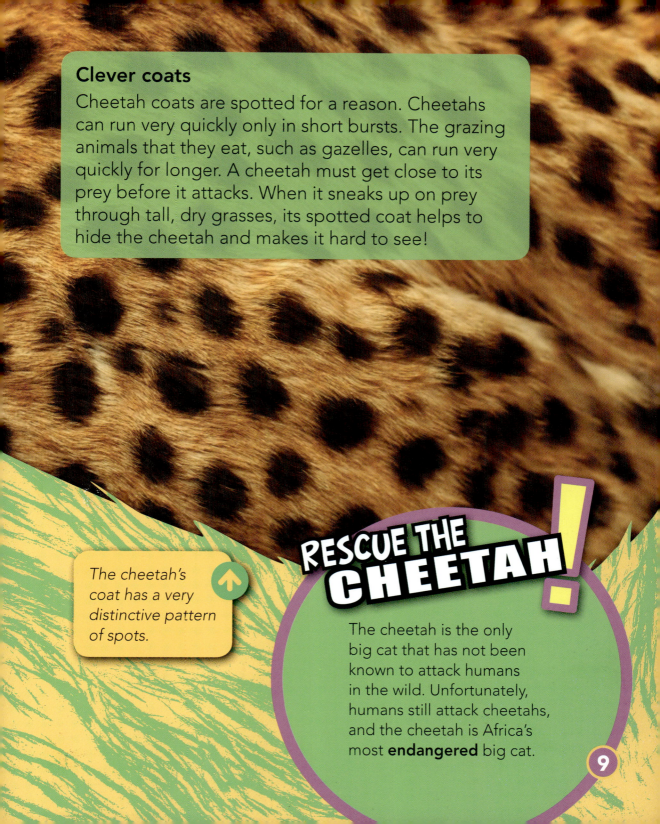

Clever coats

Cheetah coats are spotted for a reason. Cheetahs can run very quickly only in short bursts. The grazing animals that they eat, such as gazelles, can run very quickly for longer. A cheetah must get close to its prey before it attacks. When it sneaks up on prey through tall, dry grasses, its spotted coat helps to hide the cheetah and makes it hard to see!

The cheetah's coat has a very distinctive pattern of spots.

RESCUE THE CHEETAH!

The cheetah is the only big cat that has not been known to attack humans in the wild. Unfortunately, humans still attack cheetahs, and the cheetah is Africa's most **endangered** big cat.

LOSING THEIR HOMES

Today, one of the biggest dangers to cheetahs is losing their homes. Cheetahs need large areas of land to survive. However, people are taking over more and more of the land cheetahs live and hunt on every year.

More people, more land

Today, there are more people living in Africa than ever before. The rising population means that more towns and villages are needed in which to live, and extra farmland is required to grow more food. New roads cut through the grasslands, breaking up the lands where cheetahs roam and live.

Some cheetahs are killed when they try to cross roads.

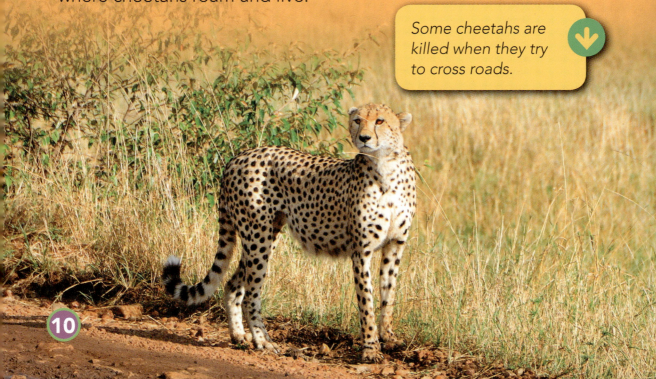

Finding food

Africa has two seasons. In the wet season, rain falls and there is a lot of grass for animals, such as gazelles, to eat. In the hot, dry season there is little rain and the grass dries up. Many grazing animals travel long distances to find grass elsewhere. Cheetahs may have to travel thousands of kilometres to find enough animals to eat.

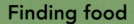

ANIMAL SOS !

Many populations of cheetahs are very small and cut off from other cheetah populations. When cheetahs are cut off from others of their kind, this increases the risk that cheetahs will die out.

Roads break up the cheetahs' open grasslands.

ENOUGH TO EAT

Cheetahs are best suited to large, open areas of land where there are lots of prey animals. In some areas, goats, cattle and other farm animals are **overgrazing** the grasslands.

The problem of overgrazing

Overgrazing is when farm animals eat the plants in one area for too long, without a break. This means the plants don't have time to grow back again. Without plants on the land, the soil becomes dry. Soil that is too dry crumbles and blows away in the wind. Then no plants can grow there. This reduces the number of animals that the cheetah can eat.

Where there is lots of grass, there are lots of gazelles for cheetahs to eat.

Hungry cheetahs

Cheetahs can see well over long distances, so they are able to spot small grazing animals to eat. They grab prey by biting it on the neck with their sharp teeth. Less than half of a cheetah's chases are successful. With fewer plants for grazing animals to eat, because of overgrazing, there are even fewer prey animals for cheetahs to eat.

RESCUE THE CHEETAH!

Organize a school event, such as a bake sale, toy sale or **sponsored** walk to raise money for a cheetah **conservation** organization.

If grazing animals move away to find food, there is less prey for cheetahs.

HUNTED!

Cheetahs are the smallest of the big cats and are of no danger to people. However, people still hunt and kill cheetahs. This happens when hungry cheetahs feed on the animals, such as sheep and goats, that villagers and farmers own.

Protecting livestock

Where there are fewer wild grazing animals to eat, some cheetahs catch farm animals instead. Farmers rely on their animals to make a living, so they trap and shoot any cheetahs that they see on their land. This is a serious problem in Namibia, an African country, where almost all of the cheetahs live on farmland.

Cheetahs sometimes catch farm animals.

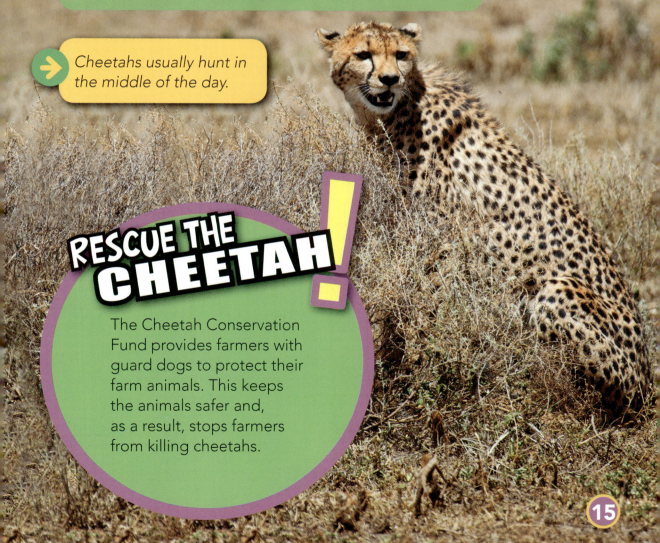

Daylight hunters

Cheetahs hunt in the daytime. The dark lines of fur under their eyes absorb sunlight, to help them see better during the day. Running uses up a lot of energy, so after a chase a cheetah needs half an hour to catch its breath before the animal can even eat. It is at this time that many cheetahs are hunted and killed by people.

→ *Cheetahs usually hunt in the middle of the day.*

RESCUE THE CHEETAH!

The Cheetah Conservation Fund provides farmers with guard dogs to protect their farm animals. This keeps the animals safer and, as a result, stops farmers from killing cheetahs.

CHANGING CLIMATE

People cause **climate change** by burning fuels such as coal, oil and gas in machines. This releases gases that build up in the **atmosphere**. The gases stop heat escaping from Earth into space. This makes Earth warmer and warmer.

Dreadful droughts

Climate change is causing more **droughts** in places such as Africa. A drought is when there is very little or no rain at all for months on end. During a drought, rivers, lakes and other water sources dry up, and the land becomes **parched**. Plants and animals then die.

Grassland animals need water sources like this one to live.

Dying of thirst

All animals need water to live. Cheetahs need to be near water and cannot survive a severe drought. In Kenya, where climate change has reduced the number of gazelles, cheetahs have been forced to feed on prey animals that aren't so good for them, such as zebra. This harms the cheetahs' health.

RESCUE THE CHEETAH!

You can help to slow climate change by using less fuel. You could share cars to school or ride your bicycle more often. You could turn off lights when you leave a room, and never leave computers or televisions on standby.

If water sources dry up, cheetahs are in trouble.

STRUGGLING TO SURVIVE

Cheetahs are not the only animals that are getting hungrier. When there are fewer grazing animals, **predators** have to compete for the food that remains. This causes problems for the cheetah.

Fighting for food

When a cheetah catches prey, other lions and leopards may fight to steal it. Cheetahs are no match for these animals. The cheetah hunts alone, while lions hunt and fight in groups. Leopards are much larger and stronger than cheetahs, too. Hungry lions and hyenas are also more likely to eat cheetah cubs.

Strong leopards steal cheetah kills.

Cheetah cubs

A female cheetah can have up to six cubs. Cubs cannot go on hunting trips until they are six weeks old, so their mother hides them in tall grass or under bushes and rocks. She moves them to a new hiding place every few days. This is a dangerous time, when nine out of ten cubs are found and killed by predators.

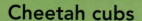

In Iran, the government is trying to protect the last remaining Iranian cheetahs by paying officers to protect cheetahs and their prey.

Female cheetahs hide newborn cubs from predators.

PARKS AND RESERVES

In some places there are **national parks** or **nature reserves** to help cheetahs. These are areas of land that are protected by law. There are rules about how people use protected land, to protect the cheetahs and other wildlife that live there.

Rules and rangers

People are not allowed to do anything that could alter the land and disturb wildlife in parks and reserves. Banned activities include farming and mining. **Park rangers** are guards with guns who patrol the parks and reserves. They look for intruders and for animal traps set by poachers.

This mother and her cub live peacefully in the Masai Mara reserve.

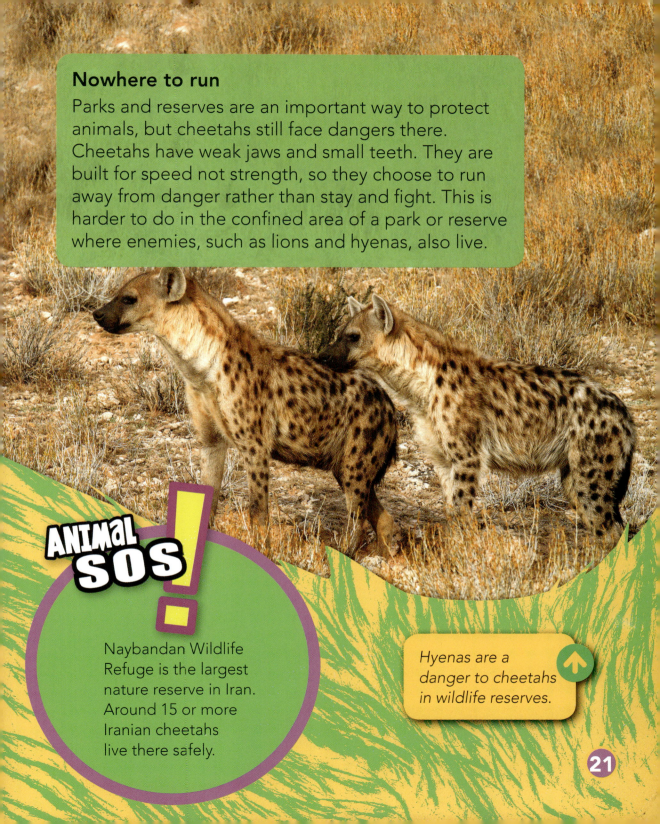

Nowhere to run

Parks and reserves are an important way to protect animals, but cheetahs still face dangers there. Cheetahs have weak jaws and small teeth. They are built for speed not strength, so they choose to run away from danger rather than stay and fight. This is harder to do in the confined area of a park or reserve where enemies, such as lions and hyenas, also live.

ANIMAL SOS!

Naybandan Wildlife Refuge is the largest nature reserve in Iran. Around 15 or more Iranian cheetahs live there safely.

Hyenas are a danger to cheetahs in wildlife reserves.

RESCUE AND RELEASE

When cheetahs are injured in fights, or harmed by poachers or farmers, they cannot catch food. This means they cannot survive alone. Cubs are also put in danger when their mother is injured or killed.

Caring for cubs

Cheetah cubs do not know how to **stalk**, pull down or kill prey when they are born. Cheetah mothers must teach their cubs these skills. Mothers bring back small, live antelopes for the cubs to catch. Later, cubs follow their mothers on hunting trips, and learn how to kill by watching the mothers hunt. If a mother cheetah is killed, her cubs will die too.

This cheetah is licking the fur of its injured brother.

To the rescue

Some organizations rescue injured cheetahs and helpless cubs. Vets treat the animals' wounds. When the cheetah is better, they release it somewhere safe, away from farmland. Cubs cannot be released into the wild because humans cannot teach cubs how to recognize and avoid predators, such as lions. Instead, rescued cubs live in special fenced reserves.

RESCUE THE CHEETAH!

Discover how you can donate money to the AfriCat Foundation. This organization rescues and helps cheetahs, and later releases them into the wild.

These cheetahs have collars because they are cared for by the AfriCat Foundation.

PROTECTING CHEETAHS

Many people across the world want to help to protect cheetahs. Some join conservation organizations that raise money to help cheetahs. Others take tourists to see cheetahs in the wild, so they will care about the future of cheetahs.

Conservation groups

People donate money to conservation organizations. The money helps to pay for food for rescued cheetah cubs. It pays for studies that investigate how to help cheetahs, and posters that tell people about what is happening to cheetahs. The money also helps pay for parks, reserves and other projects.

Many people sign up for organizations that try to help cheetahs.

Handling tourism carefully

Many tourists want to visit reserves to see cheetahs. This can help cheetahs if, for example, the money tourists pay is spent on more rangers for the parks and reserves. However, tourism must be handled carefully because cheetahs are shy creatures. Noisy tourist vehicles can disrupt their hunts, scare animals away from kills, or cause females and cubs to become separated.

Tourist jeeps must not get too close to cheetahs.

RESCUE THE CHEETAH!

Join a conservation organization, such as the World Wildlife Fund (WWF) or the Wildlife Conservation Society (WCS). You could also raise money to adopt a cheetah living in the wild.

CHEETAHS IN ZOOS

Cheetahs in zoos are very popular with visitors. They are truly beautiful creatures, and lots of people want to see the fastest land animal in the world! Do you think zoos are a good or a bad thing for cheetahs?

The good

Zoos can help cheetahs. When people see cheetahs and learn about them at zoos, they are more likely to help the animals. Unlike tigers and lions, female cheetahs mainly live alone, not in groups. They do not get lonely if kept alone in zoos. Zoos are also places where animals can raise their young safely. This could help prevent cheetahs becoming extinct in the future.

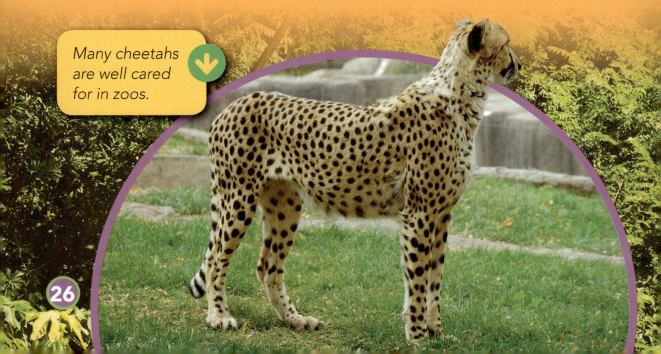

Many cheetahs are well cared for in zoos.

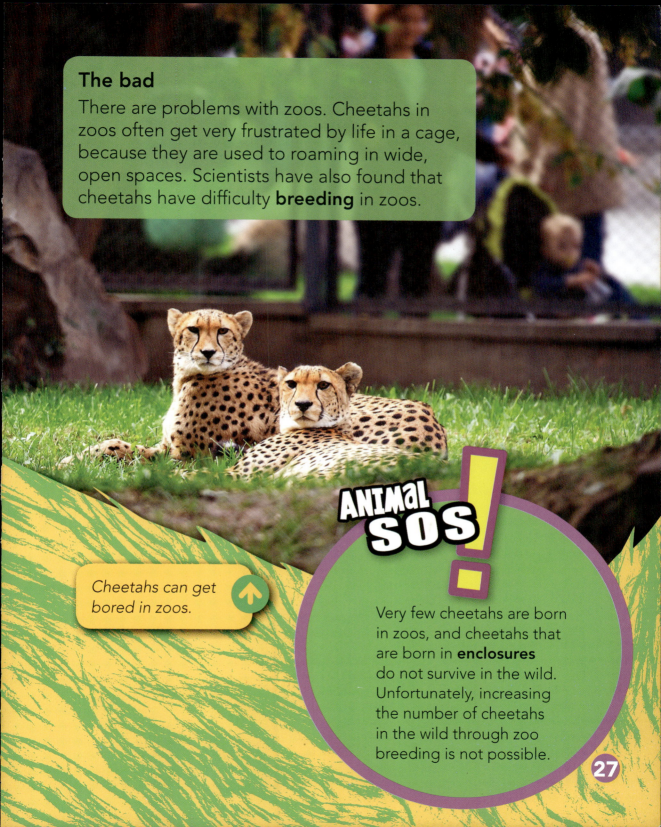

The bad

There are problems with zoos. Cheetahs in zoos often get very frustrated by life in a cage, because they are used to roaming in wide, open spaces. Scientists have also found that cheetahs have difficulty **breeding** in zoos.

Cheetahs can get bored in zoos.

ANIMAL SOS!

Very few cheetahs are born in zoos, and cheetahs that are born in **enclosures** do not survive in the wild. Unfortunately, increasing the number of cheetahs in the wild through zoo breeding is not possible.

27

WILL WILD CHEETAHS SURVIVE?

The future for cheetahs looks uncertain. All across Africa, cheetah numbers are decreasing, even within protected wildlife reserves. Will the only place to see cheetahs, in the future, be in zoos?

Scientists at work

Scientists are busy studying cheetahs in the wild and in zoos, parks and reserves. Scientists use camera traps and radio-collars to collect information about cheetahs and their needs. They study diseases that affect cheetahs to reduce the risks of illness. Scientists also find out how much space cheetahs need to survive.

Scientists study cheetahs to help them survive.

Hope for the future

Conservation organizations are making a difference, too. They are teaching local villagers, farmers and schoolchildren about the importance of cheetah conservation. More farmers now call for help to move cheetahs off their farms, rather than killing them.

Ask other people to help protect these beautiful creatures too!

RESCUE THE CHEETAH!

Spread the word! Talk to other people about cheetahs and how they need our help. The more people know about these magnificent animals, the better chance we have to save them!

GLOSSARY

atmosphere the blanket of gases around the Earth

breeding producing young

climate change an increase in the temperature of the Earth due to the release of greenhouse gases

conservation working to protect animals and the environment

droughts an unusually long period of time without rain

enclosures cages or pieces of land, which are separated from their surroundings by barriers

endangered an animal, such as a cheetah, which is in danger of becoming extinct

extinct no longer existing

grasslands large open area of country covered with grass

national parks areas of land set aside by the government of a country in order to protect the environment and wildlife that live there

nature reserves areas of land where plants and animals can live without being harmed by people

overgrazing when animals eat so many plants that the soil is dry and useless

parched very dry

park rangers people employed by a national park or nature reserve to guard and protect its wildlife

poachers people who kill wild animals illegally, usually for food or to sell parts of the animals' bodies

predators animals that kill other animals for food

prey an animal that is hunted by another animal

rudder the part on a boat that helps to steer it

sponsored giving money or support to another person to help them achieve a particular goal

stalk to creep silently and slowly towards something without being seen

FIND OUT MORE

A Day in the Life of a Cheetah, Lisa Amstutz (Raintree, 2019)

Cheetahs (Living in the Wild), Charlotte Guillain (Raintree, 2015)

Cheetahs (National Geographic Kids Readers), Laura Marsh (National Geographic Kids, 2017)

WEBSITES

10 top cheetah facts!
www.natgeokids.com/uk/discover/animals/general-animals/cheetah-facts/

More fun cheetah facts!
www.sciencekids.co.nz/sciencefacts/animals/cheetah.html

Go wild with the World Wildlife Fund kids' site!
gowild.wwf.org.uk/

INDEX